Roadkill and Joy

Arlo Carafelli

Presentation by *BookLeaf Publishing*

Web: www.bookleafpub.com

E-mail: info@bookleafpub.com

ISBN: 9789357744942

First edition 2023

To Xavier Menefee with adoration. Your support made this a reality. I love you always.

Contradictions

Constant change
and
Contrasting thoughts
When my learnt self soothing hugs and gentle
touches turns into ripping at my own skin.
Asking for change
and
Racing thoughts
When I was on top of the world and drugs were
a crutch turns into reaping my own sins.

I show people their truths and for that I'm either
a demon or a godsend.
A beautifully decrepit thing, a two month best
friend.

My problem is I'd make a great corpse and
everyone knows it.
When I was given the kiss of life death himself
had imposed it.

Confliction
Addiction
My main convictions.

When our dog died my father told me about
how it was possible to die from a broken heart.
I stopped creating art
I stopped creating art

Heart

Baby told me I'm gonna die like Elvis.
 I said gross, pick a better comparison.
 Said what's gross is how my heart's gonna pop
like that zit between your shoulder blades that
went unseen for weeks.
 But this has been seen long before it hurt this
bad.
 I have raised my palms to man and machine
 asking for help.

 Tugging and aching
 Twisting stinging pressure.
 How I imagine it would feel to be torn into by a
pack of hungry dogs.

 I've been seeing violent things happen behind
my eyes.
 How comical would it be to die over your own
mind.
 Panic, drugs, a broken heart, wine.

 "Strain on your cardiovascular system."
 *That one fucking look like you're not sure if
it's pity or fear.*

I did this to myself
You did this to me.
The chicken or the egg debate.
Maybe my father is god.
A moment of silence.

Baby told me I'm gonna die like Whitney
Houston.
i said, "Something like that."

Whisper

God baby your face.
 Baby god face.
Bring tears to my face.
Some days I want to scream love,
others I know it's bigger to whisper.
Some days I want to hold you together
even when it's because you miss her.
Others I know it's bigger to whisper.
God baby your face.
Unearthly grace.
Pink cheeks
and a smile I could never misplace.
Some days I want everyone to know our love,
others I know it's bigger to whisper.
God baby your face,
red and puffy,
tears left a trace.
Some days I want to shout to let me in,
others I know it's bigger to whisper.
A god my baby a wonder I'm in awe,
everytime I look at that face
I know it's bigger to whisper.

Woozy

6

The city in their skin.
 An abandoned tower, broken windows from
flying bricks.
 But I would love to make a home of it.
 Tight knuckles turn soft the pit in my stomach
comes out as laughter.
 I swear you saved me from several disasters.
 An angel an angel preaches the pastors.
 Compared to this angel they're all just actors.
 I love you.

Whatever's Real

Nothings real but nothing's not, delusions,
balloons infused with my vomit.
 You're dead and the man that's always three
steps to the right of me might be too.
 Looking into the screen to type is just another
open door leaking its guts out onto my floor.
 Gore.
 Fucking whore.
 Gore watches me be a fucking whore.
 My plants are doing better but the smudge in
the mirror still looks too much like myself
 and I can be alone but only with a pounding
heart.
 Fuck the man three steps to the right of me.
 I would.
 And fuck me.
 I grew up staring at the church ceiling
asking god why I am here.
 God answered, in screams.
 Yet I'm still fucking here.
 Sometimes I look at a cow and I see more.
 Sometimes I look at myself and I see less.
 I'm scared and alive and so are they.

I Am

There's another ufo over Ohio
and I am calm.
There is a train derailed chemical spill in Ohio
and I am worried.
"They shot down the spy balloon."
Well wouldn't you know it, nothing happened.
Another trans woman murdered
and I am angry.
and I am
I wasn't allowed to go to christmas because I am
a threat
and I am not
and I am.
and i feel the uneasy rise in me.
I feel it rise in the world
and I am here and I am.

The Story of the Sterile Skies

9

The sun and the moon have lived together so long, their relationship is so powerful and so strong. They created the universe and were planning to add, which made the people awfully mad. They shot a harpoon into the sky and the sun began to slowly die. The moon swiftly rushed to her side and the world's went out, sterile skies.

Cosmic Decay

Ignorance, please plague me.
I wish I was stupid, oblivious, unaware of the seriousness.
I see the violence, I can't hide from it.
It chokes me and if I die from it, well, what can I say?
I have DNR written in my DNA.
If I wasn't already doing the devil's work, I'm willing to.
If it meant I could find bliss I'd end it for all of you.
Nevermind the chaotic tone of that sentence. I'm tired of being told I'm in need of repentance.
God can't save you from the horror of humanity.
Everyone is capable of insanity.
Neither evil or good will ever win.
There's a balance between the saint and the sin.
But in the back of my mind I can't help but wonder how the good will weigh us out of this mess we're in.

The Drop

Previous codependents.
 Maybe still upset.
 Maybe I'm confusing the gut wrenching nausea
with love, the sick feeling in my chest.
 Maybe I'm fucking sick, was never not.
 Heartache, Heartbreak, blood clot.
 You have to be wrong.
 I can't be the monster that hurt you all along.
 But you're doing better now that I'm gone,
 and I'm me.
 Still can't connect.
 Still can't breath.
 Focused on how I move my feet.
 Constantly checking whats underneath.
 An inconsistent beat.
 I feel like I've been here before.
 Looking out from the shore.
 Wading in only to fall straight off the end,
 fucking gored.
 Too busy looking at what I want.
 Going straight for it,
 I didn't see the drop.

Kind

I don't feel as kind anymore,
 but I'm more myself than ever.
I have gained so much knowledge,
but I'm far less than clever.
The years have washed over me,
but my god I'm still dirty.
Mourning my old self,
hoping I make it to thirty.
Powder in my face making me less than kind.
Coughing up smoke, using the haze to keep me
blind.
Would I do it differently?
If I could go back?
Be kinder to my body.
Be kinder to my flesh.

Wizard Eyes

My lover says I have wizard eyes.
 I'd love to say he's right.
 Though the things I see aren't whimsical,
 but induce fight or flight.
 Their faces gnarled, their bodies hunched
forward, everyday is constant horror.
 I eat the ovals to make them go away,
 but they linger, they linger, they linger
 anyway.

If we Could be Ourselves

This body is a cage,
bars wide enough to slip through
only to be met with a violent gaze.
Yearning for safety.
My mind is a maze
or more like a labyrinth,
always changing my ways.
If we could be ourselves,
without fear of hate,
would we all slip more comfortably into our
fate?
If we could be ourselves,
and love our mates,
would there be more homes?
Would there be more plates?

Suffocating Grief

I can't breath.
 Agony has taken over me.
 I can scream at god all I want,
 say that I'm angry,
 it's just a front.
 Turning for hours in bed is a cunt.
 The truth is I am bad,
 even when I try to not be.
 These hands cause damage,
 turn them away from me.
 Comfort me,
 comfort me from my myself.
 Comfort me, I need help.
 What is it, I can't tell.
 Save me from this hell,
 but I can only save myself.

We Will Make It

As we hold eachother in this cold,
I see us as two dead dogs.
Wishing we could die from being old.
We are wild animals,
our passion is flammable.
Fuck the hardships we can make them
manageable.
The world around us shakes and crumbles.
Our bones brake, bellies rumble.
We have grown humble,
picking up this mess.
My darling, my love,
you look beautiful in that dress.
Let's fight the will to be depressed.
Forget those people,
yet they're still impressed.
My darling, my love,
we can make this the best.
We'll make it so we can get our rest.

Moving Along

He said looking me in the eyes is like staring
down a double barrel shotgun.
 Don't worry baby, this won't last long.
 I've been wading through this muck
 looking for where i went wrong.
 It's a song.
 Something about
 moving along.
 Life hits us one day at a time.
 It's a crime how all I can do is rhyme,
 let the dishes pile up and cry.
 It seems all I do is lie.
 But I can't keep up with what's happened in my
life.
 It's one thing after another.
 I'm a sister and a brother.
 Half the time I was under cover.
 This is me pleading to my lover.
 Please, understand how I'm me.
 Why I break so easily,
 how I move so beautifully,
 why I'm me.
 It's why I breath.

Eleanor

The rain stings like never before.
 Wet feel slapping against the floor.
 Love and joy my god I want more.
 All of my actions set me back.
 what is it for?
 It is you I adore.
 I don't want to fuck this up with the pain at my
core,
 but I'm slipping, my Eleanor.
 Losing my grip on reality.
 Baby all I can be to you is a casualty.

Molly

I feel myself in these copper lines.
Tangled and filthy,
overused, full of pride.
Took a pretty thing on a date.
She filled me with malice,
she filled me with hate,
and the next morning?
The next morning I just ached.
She got under my skin.
She got on top of the sheets.
Even back then our eyes didn't meet.
And now,
well, I am still at her feet.

It Gets Different

Life is moving, always changing.
Taking my experiences and
rearranging.
The rug swept out from under my feet again.
Here I am, still being forced to bend.
When will it end?
It doesn't.
It just gets different, my friend.